Techni

DREAMS, SUCCESS AND UNICORNS

GIULIANA CARULLO

ISBN: 978-1-9160678-0-6

To my family who daily supports my life and work.

CONTENTS

TECHNICAL LEADERSHIP
DREAMS, SUCCESS AND UNICORNS

Copyright © 2018 by Giuliana Carullo

First published: March 2019

Author: Giuliana Carullo
Editor: Michael Nolan

All opinions and concepts are my own, and by no means represent the position of any of my employers past or present.

PREFACE

PREFACE

No matter what responsibilities are in place. No matter what your job title is: software architect, senior engineer, principal engineer, project manager or CEO. They are all shades of the same abstraction: the technical leader.

We need leaders, and eventually, we want to become a really good one. Often times it is confusing still. What distinguishes a manager from a leader? What distinguishes a leader from a technical one in today tech world?

Long story short: a build up of skills and different ways to apply them.

This book is not yet another book on influencing people and on how to communicate properly. These are massively important skills, and plenty of amazing books have been already written on these topics. This book is born as a vision – often times really personal – on who a technical leader is, how he/she acts and what it takes to be a good one.

As previously said, leadership is not in title.

Leadership is talent and attitude (for the blessed) and hard work in honing a plethora of skills. This holds really true for technical leaders. Hence, in this book, we are going to focus on skills, not on job title.

This is not a teaching book. What you will get out from this book, in summary, is a - very opinionated – discussion on what makes or breaks a good technical leader. Short chapters, one step at the time.

As we walk through them you will notice a sort of role playing in place:

- myself as a technical leader;
- myself as a follower: what I look for in technical leaders that I decide to follow.

It is meant to give you some guidance, often starting from struggles that I had first to overcome myself. Furthermore, having a little of an entrepreneur soul, I spoke with myself for a fairly long time: how would it be my dream company? By which rules would I play? Hence this book was born. Think about it as a pocket guide that acts as a reminder to ourselves on how to behave in a lot of common scenarios that we face on a daily basis at work. Not because of our role: but because it is the right thing to do.

The ideas presented are backed up by easy to grasp examples showing common situations where technical leaders simply 'act differently'. Being aware of ourselves and what has been proven to work – or not to work – is the first step towards success.

Last, but not least: thank you for choosing this book. I really hope that the ideas presented will help you as much as they are helping me. Indeed, I hope that at the end of it you will be a better – or at least more conscious - leader.

TECHNICAL LEADERSHIP
DREAMS, SUCCESS AND UNICORNS

CHAPTER

LEADERSHIP

LEADERSHIP

"Remember the difference between a
boss and a leader:
a boss says go – a leader says: Let's go."

-E.M.Kelly

Managers matters. A lot. If you wondered whether or not they are needed at all. They are. It is a pretty common belief of a lot of tech people that managers only add up to increased bureaucracy and intricate communications.

Google - back in 2008 - performed an experiment to prove – or disprove – the assumption:

'Managers are Evil.'

The outcome of their research found that managers are far from being the evil force tearing down employees. They are a critical asset to the company. So the tech giant started to dig deeper and found that good managers are not only necessary, but they increase job satisfaction, retention and overall performances – if done correctly.

But more than managers we need leaders. Good Leaders. Great Leaders are even better. The two of them are not necessarily the same thing. There are many shades of managers are out there. Some of the most types overlap, whilst blurring roles are:

1. **People manager** – who often times is mainly responsible for team performances and relative interactions with the Human Resources department.
2. **Project manager** – who mainly decide schedule, risk, resources, with a touch of people management especially for smaller companies.
3. **Principal Engineer** – who, in more heavily R&D focused companies, holds the broader view of what needs to be accomplished and helps the team to reach the goals.

The separation line between people manager and the broad technical manager is often blurred. Can you be a people manager without a good technical background? Can you be a technical manager without skills like strong communication – which is often seen as an essential characteristic of a good people manager?

My personal answer is: not really. Since I have a strong background on software engineering, my view might be slightly biased by my preferences (we are all – eventually unconsciously – biased towards something). My main reasoning around it is that: the higher you go in the classical career ladder, the more the skills you have need to grow up in order to do good for yourself, your company and your team. Some of the questions I asked myself before giving you this response are:

1. What happens if you can't mentor a team member that is looking for technical guidance and mentorship?

2. Can you help someone achieve their goals towards a technical path if you don't have a grasp of the work and skills that person already has or that he/she needs to work on?

3. What happens if you can't understand someone's verbal and non-verbal communication? Would you understand that:

    a. your way of communicating something might be not well received;

    b. you are missing the main objective of the communication, which is mutual understanding;

    c. the other person is walking away unsatisfied from the chat you had?

4. Can you build trust with a person directly reporting to you if they think you have little clue or interest in what they are trying to achieve? Do they think you understand how big or complex the issue they are trying to solve is?

5. Will a direct report trust you for making decisions on his/her career if you two relate

so little on a such impactful skill – i.e., technical?

6. Can you influence and inspire people to follow you if you lack any major skill?

7. What happens if you do not have a grasp of the latest technology trends in the world?

8. What happens if you have little business knowledge?

9. What happens if you have little knowledge about customers and the competition?

10. What happens if you are too focused on the nitty-gritty technical aspects that you loose your focus on helping out team members to succeed?

11. What happens if you do not have classical project management skills? Will your projects be on track?

If you received any of my questions and comments on the personal side, please jump to the Non make it personal Chapter.

As regards the technical aspects, a broader study performed in 2016 by HBR [HBR] has actually shown that we all like managers that can do our job and that we can learn from. They are domain experts. And it holds true for engineers.

Point 6 also needs a word of caution: often times, the un-inspiring behavior is not that much to do with a 'lack of skills'. We are all human, not perfect and different. Someone has a natural talent towards certain things that someone else might compensate with other skills. And it is totally acceptable, nonetheless the beauty of the world.

Point 6 is an issue when it comes with a 'lack of desire (or ability?) to constantly improve and grow ourselves'. I believe it is fairly easy to fall in the trap of feeling comfortable with our own role and skills that we do not pay attention to how this behavior is perceived by people who surround us.

Work on your skills for yourself. The impact on others will follow. And if nothing else happens, you will be a more self-confidence and self-conscious person anyway.

TAKE AWAY

1. Managers are not Evil.

2. A technical leader has skills from classical views of technical manager, people manager and principal engineer.

3. Always work on improving yourself.

4. Don't be lazy.

CHAPTER

WHY DO YOU WANT TO BE A LEADER?

WHY DO YOU WANT TO BE A LEADER?

"Become the kind of leader that people

would follow voluntarily;

even if you had no title or position."

-Brian Tracy

So you want to be a leader. A good one. Before embarking on this lifelong journey, I would really ask you: why do you want to be one? Money? Power? Visibility? Fame? Is that a wish purely based on your ego or lack of self-confidence? Or do you feel there is much more to it?

Don't get me wrong. If you like money and power: high five! And I wish you all the best. What I am really trying to say here is: can you really see yourself as a leader apart from an imagined future picture you have of yourself?

Let's say you see yourself as a Principal Engineer sometime in the future, are you purely in love with the idea of being one? And most importantly are you aware what it is all about? Are you willing to do what it takes to be there?

Think about it, please. And don't put yourself in a miserable position – which by all means is any sort of situation inside and outside of work that will make you wake up everyday like it was a big, infinite Monday morning.

Far away from discouraging you. I am your biggest fan if you are trying to be a leader to impact the world with the greatness inside you. And I really think that your life will be better in general by mastering some core skills commonly associated with leaders. My question wants to specifically solicit thoughts around: I want to be a CEO. Yes. But why?

A common wisdom for leaders who want to accomplish their work and life goal is to:

"visualize yourself."

It is a widely applied concept which is based on the principle that using visualization is a motivating experience to boost productivity and move faster towards goals.

What I suggest here is to visualize yourself with all the pros and cons of what you wish to become. Does a detailed view of yourself matches the more platonic view of a technical leader?

TAKE AWAY

1. Don't do it just for the money or fame.

2. Visualize yourself. Not only to motivate yourself. Do it to understand if being a technical leader is what you really want

3. Find out how do you fit the world and what makes you happy.

CHAPTER

LEADERSHIP PRINCIPLES OF TECH GIANTS

LEADERSHIP PRINCIPLES OF TECH GIANTS

"Innovation distinguishes between
a leader and a follower."

-Steve Jobs

As part of their research on managers, Google launched the Project Oxygen [Project Oxygen] – and made their findings publicly available about what it means to be a great manager at Google. Top skills and highlighted behaviors are:

- Good coach
- Empowering teams and do not micromanage
- Creating an inclusive team environment, showing concern for success and well-being
- Productive and results-oriented
- Good communicator - listens and shares information
- Supporting career development and discussing performance
- Clear vision/strategy for the team
- Having key technical skills to help advise the

team
- Collaboration across Google
- Strong decision maker

Also Amazon made its Leadership Principles available [Amazon Principles]. What constitute a good leader at Amazon is:

- Customer Obsession
- Ownership
- Invent and Simplify
- Are Right, A Lot
- Learn and Be Curious
- Hire and Develop the Best
- Insist on the Highest Standards
- Think Big
- Bias for Action
- Frugality
- Earn Trust
- Dive Deep
- Have Backbone; Disagree and Commit
- Deliver Results

A lot of core skills for a leader are actually in common, but what do they mean in our day-to-day work?

Some of them are more obvious, like deliver results. What about the others? As an example, what does being a good coach mean? For sure we can all nod happily thinking about a leader who is a good coach, possibly with good presentation and communication skills. I am

100% sure that 99.9% of us have on our CV:

'good communication and presentation skills'

or similar. But are good mentors all created equally? What do they have in common? What makes a technical leader instead of a motivational speaker?

Another related point that I spent some time reflecting on - inspired by findings and company cultures - is: given the higher-level policies and guidance is our team healthy? Are we able - as technical leaders - to use what is known to be good to look for conflicts and dysfunctionalities in our team?

Assumption: conflicts are positive if properly approached. Consider two software engineers, each of them with a different style to perform the same task. They might avoid conflict at all and keep working independently without speaking each other. Can you enable communication between the two and agree with them a common way to proceed?

Are you recognizing conflicts which instead should not happen? A pretty common example is a team where members are not free to speak up their ideas, or teams that are not open to embrace new changes. The scenario is the following: Joe is super engaged, always ready to present new ideas, technologies, tools, you name it. But he, more often than not, is immediately shot down without the possibility to give a reasoning about his proposal. "That's stupid", "that wouldn't work", "we don't care about that". What will start to happen soon is that Joe and other team members will stop proposing possible improvements and they loose engagement.

As technical leaders, we are called upon recognizing this mismatch between how it is supposed to be and what it is in reality and enable a better environment, for ourselves and our teams.

In the following Chapters, we will keep on addressing, with practical scenarios, which traits and capabilities make a good technical leader.

TAKE AWAY

1. Are you able to track and enforce company guidelines and culture?

2. Do you recognize dysfunctionalities within the team?

3. Do you promptly act to stop them?

THE TECHNICAL LEADER DIAGRAM

THE TECHNICAL LEADER DIAGRAM

"Leadership and learning
are indispensable to each other."

-John F. Kennedy

I like to look at the Technical Leader as the mythological creature that owns major (hard and soft) skills from the three worlds:

- Project Management
- People Management
- Technical Skills

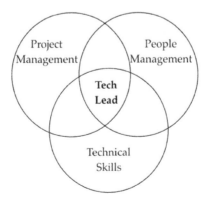

The Technical Leader should have the perspective and capabilities of the classic Project Manager:

- time,
- budget and
- project quality management

the soft skills of a People Manager:

- communication,
- influence,
- care for direct reports' career;

and the background and attitude of technical people – call them nerds if it helps in clarifying the view – who constantly challenge themselves to learn technical stuff. Sure enough, a technical leader might not deal with coding on a daily basis. But rest assured that he/she is still current on technologies and how the world around him/her is evolving.

As an addition, I would suggest to work on your skills as a salesperson. It does not matter if in your specific role you do not relate with customers directly. You are the seller of yourself, your work, your brand and your ideas. This doesn't mean that you have to be constantly bragging about how good your work is. Don't do that. It is a sort of cold calling to put it into the words of the sales field. And I believe it does not really work out. How many times we get bored about people who's only topic is "me"?!

I am a strong believer that your work should speak by itself, and it will with a little patient, constancy of the effort and the amazingness you put into your job. However, never speaking about the work you do is unforgiving. You should be able to stand up for your work and speak about it with no hesitation. Skills in sales will help you in learning the right way to voice your message and have people listening and hopefully buying into it.

As Professor Jordan Peterson [Peterson] said in several of his talks:

"You better grow teeth"

His dissertation is around building up some toughness in your personality, because if you are not capable of this, you will end up being the victim of others who actually can. He remaps the general idea to martial arts, where they teach you how to eventually fight but they do not train you to fight. Martial arts teach how to be peaceful and have capabilities under control. If you happen to be in a fight, however, you know how to defend yourself.

The same applies to your job. You don't have to brag, but you have to grow your teeth to defend your work. Finding the right balance between bragging and speaking up is not easy. Being more on the 'my work will speak for me' side, I struggled myself to reach this balance. But it is a necessary evil in order to be heard in such a competitive world.

TAKE AWAY

1. Build your Project Management skills.

2. Build your People Management skills.

3. Keep your interest for technical stuff high. Be current on what is happening in the world.

4. Become a salesperson.

5. Grow some teeth.

CHAPTER

IT'S ALL ABOUT TRUST

IT'S ALL ABOUT TRUST

"Leadership is the phenomenon of someone
following someone else because they want to,
not because they have to."

-Larry Wilson

If people don't trust you, you can hardly influence them and be a leader. People are not going to trust and follow you just for the sake of your title. Neither will they do it based on your charisma alone. For a technical leader – hence mainly playing in the engineering field - this means that:

- your technical contributions are evident;
- you are most of the time a high-performer;
- you are held accountable for your work;
- you hold others accountable for their work;
- you do not seek undeserved credits;
- you give credits every time it is needed to do so;
- your team can trust you to hold their back;
- you create a transparent and collaborative environment around you;

- integrity;
- clear communication;
- don't be a narcissist;
- don't deliberately damage the careers of others to build your own;
- you promote success, not average results;
- don't point your finger at others faults;
- don't lie;
- trust others by default. If proven wrong, give a second chance but explain exactly what went wrong and what needs to be fixed.

That is a lot of stuff. And probably much more should be pointed out. Building trust takes time. And during this time you need to show the people around you that you own all the right ingredients.

Be aware, anyway, that the more responsibilities you have, the easier it is to break trust. Certain things are easy to fix, little misunderstandings or miscommunications. If they happen once, twice at most. If people can sense a pattern of 'miscommunication' they will not trust you anymore, probably ever.

Certain things are more impactful than others. If you take undeserved credits for the work of others, or you don't recognize the work of others, people will probably give you a second chance to rectify with no hesitation. If you do it constantly – especially in case of lack of contributions – you will have lost all your hard-gained respect with that person.

If you lie, you lost your game immediately. That person you lied to will hardly believe any other single word you could say on the topic. Regaining trust is not impossible, but even harder.

Behave! Behave! Behave! Nothing works better than leaders that consistently model their words through actions. If you proclaim your company culture, but you don't act upon it yourself, your team will not trust you. Be accountable for what you say you are going to do. And do not procrastinate.

Let's consider another general scenario. Robert asked you to help him out to solve an issue he is going through at the moment. You kindly agreed that you will let him know when things will be done. Robert waits with plenty of hopes and gratitude for your help. A week pass by, and Robert receives no response. He follows up with you, but you excuse yourself: too busy. Robert waits, probably with little less hope. What happens if you keep on procrastinating? Robert will loose his trust in you.

We can get too busy prioritizing other responsibilities that we forget simple tasks that can build trust with other people. Would you be happy with Robert if you ask him to help on a task and he replies: "yes, I will let you know"?

Well, probably not really.

TAKE AWAY

1. Trust is the number one rule for being a technical leader.

2. Without trust you can't influence people.

3. Certain behaviors are worst than others.

4. If you lie, you are out of the game.

5. Lead by example.

CHAPTER

AND LOYALTY

AND LOYALTY

"You've got to give loyalty down,

if you want loyalty up."

-Donald T. Regan

As human beings we love loyalty: it makes us feel safe and comfortable. As I grew up, I had a much stronger sense of how much the pocket influences behavior. And it is reasonable. Let me explain better. Yes, we love to be on a mission, have a purpose in life and to work on something that we like and we care for, but it won't pay the bills.

And the exact same concept applies to a company: you can be a lovely person, but at the end of the day is all about: how much money the company earns because of your work. That's fair enough.

Due to this general truth, often the focus is heavier on customers rather than employees (your team).

Customers and the team are two faces of the same coins: you need to equally care about both. Your customers are going to pay the bill. But your people is are going to create the billable assets that customers want to pay for.

And as you like to feel safe with a loyal employee, you need to pass down loyalty first. You really can't keep asking the best of others without giving the best of yourself first. Neither can you ask for loyalty with a promise that one day you will be loyal to them.

Little note: we are not speaking about unicorns here. As I said: money influences our behavior and it always will. But healthy work relationships will impact much more on our behaviors. It is widely known that the majority of people leave a job because of a "bad boss". And loyalty has a lot to do with a bad or good leader. If your people can sense that you are not loyal to them, that you don't value the work and sacrifices they put into their job, they are going to leave, period.

You can't really complain then if your team is not loyal to you as you have not been loyal to them. All relationships are about reciprocation, and if people leave the job you probably missed this point.

TAKE AWAY

1. Do you reciprocate loyalty?

2. Do you care more about who pays the bills rather than who creates for you the bills that people wants to pay?

CHAPTER

HUMBLE AND CARING

HUMBLE AND CARING

"Fullness of knowledge always and necessarily means some understanding of the depths of our ignorance, and that is always conducive to both humility and reverence."

-Robert A. Millikan

We have to have a depth of expertise as technical leaders as we discussed in the Leadership Chapter.

At the cost of expressing an obvious fact: we do not know everything. Even if we are expert in the things we do. Repeat with me:

"I am an expert, but I do not know everything."

Once we have fully metabolized it, we are closer to being a good leader. Always have the humility and courage to allow yourself to benefit from the expertise of others. No matter if they are below you in the company's hierarchy. Remember, it is not about the title. If you already do it, but based on a merely selfish attitude (i.e., you reuse other's ideas and knowledge for your and only your benefit go back to the Trust Chapter.

Let's consider an example of being open to listen to new ideas, whilst being a selfish 'leader'.

> **Mark**: "So I had the idea X, which I think the company might benefit from."
>
> **Manager**: " Ok, go on… "
>
> **Mark**: "Well, I prototyped an initial version, and I had good results. Indeed…" [showcasing the results]
>
> **Manager**: "That's great Mark, I really like it! Can you follow up with more details?"
>
> **Mark**: "Of course I can. I will share as soon as possible."

What happens after a while is that, instead of giving back credit and supporting Mark's idea, our manager is the only person aware of Mark's work. Indeed, whenever possible, the manager supports Mark to keep working on it, whilst giving very little credits to Mark.

This is not humble, nor courageous behaviour. You could do worse: not listening at all, pretending to know the absolute truth about the world and its facts.

Again:

> "I am an expert, but I do not know everything."

We really do not have to repeat why not giving credit is so bad. But we can do even better:

- ask if you can help out, from a genuine interest, and act upon it if help needed;
- create an open environment where people feel safe, engaged and gratified for sharing their ideas;
- respect all the people surrounding you. In this context you show respect by:
    - challenging everyone's ideas (yes also your superiors' ones);
    - welcoming ideas from everybody (yes, especially from people 'below' you);
    - not being severely biased (e.g., this person in my opinion knows more than this other one on that specific topic).

TAKE AWAY

1. Be humble and caring.

2. At the cost of a totally wanted repetition: give credit where credit is due!

3. Do not fake an open-minded and caring attitude for your own benefit: you will be quickly called out loosing the hard gained trust.

IF YOU CAN'T MANAGE YOUR TIME HOW WILL YOU MANAGE YOUR TEAM?

IF YOU CAN'T MANAGE YOUR TIME HOW WILL YOU MANAGE YOUR TEAM?

"Lack of direction, not lack of time, is the problem.
We all have twenty-four hour days."

-Zig Ziglar

The term manage in the title can be somehow misleading. Once again it is not about micromanaging. Interpret it in the light of: how can you help others to have their work all put together if yours is not?

Becoming a technical leader is for sure no joke. It requires tons of commitment and probably also a bunch of sacrifices. But how many times do we see 'leaders' who do not have enough time for themselves, for family, for having a bare minimum of a life outside of the office.

Balance is not an option. Getting busier at times is ok, deadlines and responsibilities kick in here and there. But if you are busy all the time, there is no way to have some time for yourself, weekends included, something is seriously wrong. How can we achieve a healthy work/

life balance? By working at best during work hours.

The most popular excuses I heard so far are:

1. Too many clients.
2. My team constantly needs my help, is not autonomous.
3. If I am not here for a half an hour everything will crash.
4. You don't get the point; you don't have the same responsibilities I have.

And the list could grow much longer. Nope, your team will not die if you are not in for an hour. And if it hypothetically does, you might not have the right resources in your team. You might be too much controlling. You might not trust your team to get the job done. You might not provide enough mentorship to someone in the team to grow up their capabilities.

In the end, instead of searching for excuses, focus on:

1. how to better manage your time to get the most out of the working hours;
2. the root cause of constantly not having enough time.

And in the end, let's remember: we will be on earth for a limited time. Sad story short. While we want to leave our legacy as leaders and have a positive impact on the world, we surely don't want that our bad time management and decisions will make our life, and the life of those who surround us, worst rather than fulfilling and joyful.

However, a word of caution is needed. At times, it does not matter how efficiently you work during work hours, it will always eat into your personal time if you let it. You have to have the discipline that when you go home, tonight, you will not open your laptop, you will spend your time that you are not paid for with family, with friends, relaxing, exercising, doing something that makes you happy and gives to others in your life.

Repeat with me:

"The company does not care about me. I am not important to them. The people I am important to are my friends and family."

Have the strength to close the laptop and say, no, the company can wait, there is only so much of my life that I allow them to have in return for a salary. If the works piles up, it is the company's problem and resources or replanning has to be done so that work can be completed in a reasonable time and employees can actually relax and switch off when not in the office.

TAKE AWAY

1. If you can't effectively manage your time, how can you manage others?

2. Not enough time: get your stuff together. There is something else which is wrong.

3. Better manage your time to get the most out of the working hours.

4. What is the root cause of constantly not having enough time?

CHAPTER

HAVE A VISION AND KNOW HOW TO COMMUNICATE IT

HAVE A VISION AND KNOW HOW TO COMMUNICATE IT

"A leader has the vision and conviction

that a dream can be achieved.

He inspires the power and energy to get it done."

-Ralph Lauren

Leadership has very little to do as we already said with titles. And it has even less in common with the authority which has been given to you. You are a leader if you build every day your authority and people follow you based on what they have seen of you.

During the process you should definitely:

1. Develop you vision
2. Communicate it
3. Inspire and help people
4. Inspire people towards achieving it.

Do you have a mission? Do you have a vision that you want to achieve and do you need help to make it happen? If not, we are missing the roots of the tree and we are just speaking about the leaves. If you don't have a mission and a vision, go back on "Why do you want to be a Leader?" Chapter. If you don't have a burning motivation and clear goals yourself, other people will hardly understand or randomly follow you.

You probably went back, wrote down on a piece of paper what you want to achieve and what motivates you. Welcome back.

Can you synthetically and passionately formulate what your vision is? If not, do a little bit of extra work. Probably your vision is not clear enough to allow you to communicate it to people who surround you.

Don't try to be a leader on something just because there is a gap. As an example, nowadays we all speak about Machine Learning and Artificial Intelligence (AI) and how it is transforming our society. Let's say Mary picks as her mission:

'I want to transform the way we do healthcare by means of AI.'

Can you see what is not working in this mission statement? For sure it is too vague. Healthcare is definitely too broad. What do you want to achieve there? What drives you in that space? What are your strengths and beliefs that make you the right person to achieve that goal? Are you choosing AI and healthcare just because of their hype in today's tech world? This is a recipe for disaster. Even if you end up building something out of it, you might end up in not being happy with what you delivered for the world. It simply does not motivate you. As Theodore M. Hesburgh said:

"The very essence of leadership
is that you have to have vision.
You can't blow an uncertain trumpet."

Once you have all set up, speak about your vision, what you are passionate about. Don't feel intimidated by giving a name and a voice to your thoughts. Play your trumpet and do it often. Don't be scared to speak about your mission, and if someone does not want to listen, they might simply not have the same passions, keep going, be patient, and your voice will be heard.

At this point you should have someone who believes in you and is willing to follow and help you out. Do you take their help for granted? No. You can't and you will not. Be grateful for what you did so far and give back. People are following you, are helping you out and you are obliged to help them back.

Leadership is not a one-way path. Keep in engaging and listening. We are all a little selfish and that's human nature. People are helping you out, but won't do it if you don't give back by means of: appreciation, gratitude and care for their goals. No one can win, without the help of the other.

Finally, it is time to provide your clear guidance in order to achieve that vision. Little word of caution from Murphy:

"things will go wrong in any given situation,

if you give them a chance. "

Be proactive and anticipate risks. Control the situation (not people) by turning bad or not-that-desired things into opportunities rather than responding after to the consequences of letting go in the hope of everything working out wonderfully by itself.

Before progressing on other traits and behavior of a good technical leader, let me provide you another bad situation that can happen if you do not have or communicate properly your vision.

Consider Oliver: a technical leader who is supervising 5 different projects with relative teams. He struggled a bit to communicate his vision and to make sure that all people are aligned with the goal of their own project as well as the bigger vision. He also does not really proactively anticipate risks. What if people on different teams end-up doing redundant work? This is not really the best utilization of resources.

TAKE AWAY

1. Develop you vision. If you don't have one, what do you want to lead?

2. Is your vision too broad?

3. Communicate it, and know how to do it effectively

4. Inspire and help people.

5. Inspire people towards achieving your vision.

6. Be proactive and anticipate risks.

CHAPTER

LISTEN, OBSERVE AND ACT UPON IT

LISTEN, OBSERVE AND ACT UPON IT

"The pessimist complains about the wind.

The optimist expects it to change.

The leader adjusts the sails."

-John Maxwell

A leader who notice that something is not working out, no matter at which level he/she operates, will not stop at the complain phase.

Let's deal with a common example in the technical world: that piece of software that always breaks, not well documented, difficult to extend, you name it. It is so easy to just complain about how poorly written it is and to point at someone else's flaws:

- Henry does not care about code quality.
- Li never writes comments.
- Lia always leave things unfinished.
- Can we simply rewrite it? John would you rewrite the entire code?

Leadership is also taking a chance to improve things that do not work properly. Even if nobody else wants to do them. You are doing the right thing, and that's all that matters. Be the person who sits down and improve things. Be the person who passionately does the rights things even it is not the easiest thing to do.

And if you are the leader of a leader, allow them to do good. No matter if they care about technical debt, operational processes, innovation. Give them a chance. Don't put limits on them. They are doing good for their careers, your own and the company overall.

Little notice: take the risk to do right even if the importance of what you are doing is not already recognized by people around you. But be ready to motivate what you are doing and why you are doing. Especially with who is supposed to accept or not the work you do. That's easier for them and for yourself if you have a clear view of the broad spectrum of the changes you are proposing and implementing. Show that your decisions are well-though out, not just an impulse.

TAKE AWAY

1. Do not complain: fix things.

2. Take the risk to do the right thing even if people around you do not recognize it right now.

3. If you are the leader of a leader: don't put limits on him/her.

CHAPTER

EXPECTATIONS

EXPECTATIONS

"Leaders instill in their people a hope for success and a belief in themselves. Positive leaders empower people to accomplish their goals."

-Unknown

No matter if the team member is more autonomous or if he/she needs more guidance towards setting up goals (short/medium/long term and career-wise), clear expectations are an absolute must have.

A lack of expectations is a lose-lose situation for all involved: the company, the employee and yourself as a manager. Not setting clear expectations is a Pandora's box. This is what happens if you fail to set a target for your team:

1. Lack of engagement.
2. Underperforming or overworked team.
3. Deadlines are missed.
4. Unclear risk assessment.
5. No career-growth.
6. Economic loss.
7. High turnover.

8. Conflicts in the team.

Let's analyze the case of the super-career oriented team member, let's call her Lucy. Often, this type of person is really self-conscious. Autonomous employees require little guidance on the actual job, whilst she needs more guidance on the long term and feedbacks on how to improve as a professional.

This is the case where we might be temped to neglect to set expectations, because Lucy always strives for success and achieves more and more. She is doing good for the entire team and the company. Which is true. But it does not work in the long run.

Without clear expectation, it will be unnecessarily difficult for you and Lucy to have even simple discussions on her performances. It will create also an undermining dissatisfaction on Lucy's part, which – based solely on her official title, might find difficult to navigate in her career-progression. She is doing a lot – and often you can see it clearly – but she has no sense of what constitutes a good impact, what makes you happy about her job, and what will help her progress in her career. Over time, you will likely see a lack of engagement and an overworked person, all due to missing vision on the value her work is providing to the company and how she can achieve her personal work goals.

This will negatively impact – of course – on the company: low retention, difficulties in meeting internal goals and monetary losses.

Let's analyze the other extreme of the spectrum: the little Bob. Bob needs a little more guidance on what is required out of him on his daily job. Maybe he has not his career-goals all in place, he needs help on planning his work, or he simply is a little bit lazy. Whatever the case is, not providing Bob's expectations does not do him nor the company a favor. In the worst case, you would end up with all the negative impacts listed above.

Let's consider you: the manager/leader. Would you be comfortable to clearly set deadlines and have them matched if you have no clue on what the team is up to? Will you be able to provide fair performance assessments? I guess the honest response on both of these is: no. Far away from micromanaging, this is another beast that we will fight later on in the book.

As a final world, failure to set clear expectations might create totally avoidable conflicts within the team.

Going back to Lucy and Bob. They work in the same team. Even in the best case, where Lucy only just tries to do the best at her job – let's assume no bad intentions - and Bob is trying to do his best – even if he is a little bit confused on what he needs to actually do (no bad intentions again) – weird feelings might be in place between the two. Who will be the person responsible for a success? Who will hold accountable for decisions or if something goes wrong?

I can read your mind:

'That's team work, the team wins or the team loses.'

In an ideal world, with plenty of unicorns, yes I agree. In the real world, it really does not work that way. I have never seen an entire team getting a promotion at the end of the year, neither an entire team fired.

TAKE AWAY

1. Not setting clear expectations is a Pandora's box.

2. Unclear expectations create conflicts.

3. Both not existing expectations and ambiguous ones are a loose-loose scenario.

CHAPTER

DON'T MAKE IT PERSONAL UNLESS IT IS IN THE PRAISE YOU GIVE

DON'T MAKE IT PERSONAL UNLESS
IT IS IN THE PRAISE YOU GIVE

"The challenge of leadership is to be strong,

but not rude;

be kind but not weak; be thoughtful but not lazy;

be humble but not timid; be proud but not arrogant;

have humor but without folly."

-Jim Rohn

First thing first: can you handle criticism and constructive feedbacks? If not, find a way to learn to do so. Constructive feedback will make you grow.

Set up your surrounding environment to boost your feedback. Appreciations of our work results in happiness for the soul, but lessons learned and feedbacks on what we can improve are priceless. The comments received from upper management, peers and eventually reports are all equally important.

Ask for feedback, stay humble and be really open to listen carefully, even if at first you might think that you received an unfair comment. There is always room for improvement. And even if what you hear is not objectively true, it might be the case that something else is lacking. To better understand what I mean here, let's consider the case of Jim. Jim supervises a team of 10 people, including Patrick. In one of their conversations, Patrick points out that he feels discouraged and not appreciated. Two things can happen:

1. Jim takes the comment a little bit on the personal side, he is trying his best to make all people happy. How can Patrick not see that? He also received a pretty big pay raise recently.

2. Jim encourages a more engaging conversation to actually find and fix the root cause.

What might be really happening in this situation is that the two of them need to work on their communication skills. Maybe, the true issue Patrick has is that he would like a thank you here and there, which is taken for granted by his manager.

Getting defensive, never pays off. Always engage to better understand what's going on, other than what appears to be on the surface of the words said. What is the real feedback and hook for improvement?

On the other side, also communicating feedback as a leader – especially the "negative" ones - should be done with care.

What not to do:

1. Always saying it is all good. That's nice to know that our job is appreciated, but we are not perfect and we know that. A lot of times we want to progress and employees really need your feedback and guidance as a leader.

2. Do not set in place comparisons between people, especially if you are doing it for the purpose of encouraging the person you are speaking with. Comparisons do not do you or any of the people involved in a favor. Indeed, not only can this behavior can create conflicts and potential resentment in the team, but it is not really working towards your goal: motivating people.

Instead, appreciation and constructive feedback needs to be:

1. Timely. which means as soon as humanly possible. As an example, if something happened during a meeting, giving feedback soon after it or the day after will work.

2. Clear and specific. Be really specific with was ok or not ok. Otherwise, for constructive feedback, the other hand might not have a good understanding of which situation or behavior needs to be stopped. For positive reinforcement, the unclear or too generic appreciations might be not really effective.

3. Non-judgmental. Don't be wishy-washy in order

to avoid conflicts. But don't be judgmental or engaging in any passive-aggressive or manipulative behavior.

4. Provide a follow up. Follow up are perfect for providing expectations. For example: "hence, we need to fix this specific aspect" or "thus, we can work on this by..." or "I do expect that...", will work nicely to set and encourage the behavior that it is supposed to happen as a consequence of the given feedback.

You can think of using SBI (Situation Behavior Impact) framework. Or any other well-know framework of your choice. But the little rules above are mandatory.

As a final note: if your team feels it is easier to win Nobel prizes rather than get recognition from within the company, something is tremendously. Do not procrastinate solving this issue: you might end up with a singleton team: you.

TAKE AWAY

1. Learn how to receive constructive feedbacks.

2. Learn how to give constructive feedbacks.

3. If your team feels it is easier to win Nobel prizes rather than get recognition from within the company, something tremendously wrong is in place.

CHAPTER

MICRO-
MANAGING

MICROMANAGING

"When I give a minister an order,

I leave it to him to find the means

to carry it out."

-Napoleon Bonaparte

Do you want to have the last word upon absolutely everything? Think about it twice.

You are a micromanager if:

- You need to be on top of absolutely everything.
- Everything needs to go through your hands and under your eyes.
- There is one and only one way to do the job: yours.
- You underestimate deadlines based on your ego: I could do it faster and better.
- You constantly look after people. Not for a genuine attitude to enquiry for any help needed. It is just because of the controlling attitude.
- You tell your team what needs to be achieved,

but you also tell them how to do their job.

- If you look deeper inside you, you are a little insecure about yourself.
- Your team clearly said you are micromanaging.
- Nobody can make decisions – even small ones – without asking to you first.

You don't need to really know anything and decide everything. Learn how to mentor people and delegate responsibilities. There is no single way to do things. Trust your team to do good. It is highly probable they will produce much more than what you were expecting.

Often people not only knows how to do the job (you hired them because of that, remember?!) but they also know the what. Trust them and be keen to also follow their directions. Know your people better to understand how they work and in which conditions they actually work at their best. It is about them, not just you.

Micromanaging is bad, period. The best that can happen is that they will stop sharing their talent and quickly become disengaged. Worst case if you happen to micromanage a will-be leader. The will-be leader - or the leader-under-cover - will be out of the company at the speed of light.

The micromanaged team will soon start to loose trust and gang up against you, with bad consequences for you and the project they are working. You've been warned.

TAKE AWAY

1. Are you allowing your insecurities to make you act as a micromanager?

2. Your team needs guidance and mentorship, not a laundry list of things that need be done.

CHAPTER
COMMUNICATION

COMMUNICATION

"The art of communication
is the language of leaders."

-James Humes

As I said in the Preface: this is not a book on strategies for effective communication. There is a concept – however – that I'd like to walk you through that I think will make the difference in how your message is perceived by your team: the why, how, what pattern.

The majority of us are well versed into the opposite pattern: what, how, why. It is the easiest one and often times agreed as a standard way to explain task and concepts. As an example, research papers are often approached this way:

"In this paper, we solve the issue X (what),
by means of providing new algorithms based on Y
(how). By doing that we demonstrate that… which is
really important in order to…(why)"

Fill in blanks with your preference. Even if it conveys well all the steps undertaken, it is not optimal to keep the reader engaged, motivated and willing to buy into that idea.

By reversing how we normally present our ideas, we can be more effective communicators. This is especially true for the interactions within the team. This pattern relates well with what we discussed in Have a vision and know how to communicate it Chapter.

A possible scenario is the following:

Manager: "Jane, I'd like you to work on feature X in the next Sprint."

Jane: "Ok, what about the acceptance metrics of X?"

Manager: "Well, for this feature we really care about user acceptance, the deadline we have with our customer Z is very close and we need to make sure that what we are delivering matches their expectations."

Jane: "Ok, I'll do that.".

Jane sighs and she hopes she'd be out of work soon.

A better way to imprint the same discussion would be:

Manager: "Jane, you know that our deadline with customer Z is really close: two weeks' time. Our main mission here is to match their expectations, and I think your contribution can be of high impact towards this goal."

Jane: "Oh cool! How can I help with that?"

Manager: "Well, we want to make sure that we pass acceptance tests of feature X by the end of this Sprint."

Jane: "I can do that."

Manager: "That's perfect Jane, let me know if you need some help out of me."

Jane: "Thanks!"

Can you tell why the second style works better than the first one?

First, the manager clearly set the expectations and starts with the why something is needed from Jane. He also seizes the opportunity to show that he trusts Jane. Then, he moves to the how (acceptance tests) and the what (feature X). Our manager – however - does something more: he offers his help in case of something needed, setting up Jane for a successful execution.

Jane feels energized. She understands the importance of her work and the task assigned to her. She also feels comfortable in asking for help in case needed and she is confident enough of her manager covering her back.

TAKE AWAY

1. Try to use the why, how, what patter to improve your communication style.

2. When assigning tasks, take a chance to explain the importance of the contribution and how it aligns with the overall goal.

THE HAPPY TECHNICAL LEADER

THE HAPPY TECHNICAL LEADER

"The single biggest way to impact an organization
is to focus on leadership development.
There is almost no limit to the potential
of an organization
that recruits good people, raises them up as leaders
and continually develops them."

-John Maxwell

The need to know principle does not always work. In the world of Information Security, the need to know principle limits the kind and the amount of information that a subject (person or system) can access in order to carry out his or her responsibilities. While perfectly grounded and holding true in the security field, applying it to the information shared within the team is not the best route to success.

Give everyone the same opportunity. The missing for a person in terms of career growth might be a better understanding of what the senior leaders are thinking about.

Having transparent, clear and timely pass-downs is a win-win scenario. The worst that can happen is that lazy employers would not care and put that information into the forgive immediately box. The best scenario is having a team that act like children unwrapping Christmas gifts.

This is a big chance – indeed - for those fully invested in growing with the company. These people, our future leaders, will use this magnificent tool you gave them as a Swiss Army knife. It will allow them to better understand your vision and contribute much more. It will also them to have their opinion and they will challenge the status quo as a consequence: such a powerful tool for growth. You would be a happier leader.

TAKE AWAY

1. Need to know principle does not apply to pass-downs.

2. Give everyone the same opportunity.

3. Make your pass-downs transparent, clear and timely.

CHAPTER

ON LIMITS

ON LIMITS

"Do not allow anybody to tell you
what your limits are."

-me

Do not allow anybody to tell you what your limits are. Do not allow anybody to set a threshold for what great things you can achieve in your life.

It is very easy to focus on our weaknesses and to allow them to take control over our mood. Weaknesses are only a tool for grandness if conveyed correctly. There is a need for a subtle, whilst important, change in mindset: be aware of weaknesses, fully embrace them and work to improve. However, be grateful for your strengths and what you achieved. Keep going and do good whenever you can.

There has been a period of my life when I felt insecure. But it has always been a weird feeling. Initial insecurities have always been paired with the burning willingness to do more with my passion for science. And after a couple of decades after that very first day that I decided to be a computer scientist, that fire isn't gone away. But I recognized that my desire to do more was my source of insecurities: I want to be 1000 but I did only 10 so far.

What I learned, and I hope you will too, is to not allow that inner voice in search for more to discourage your soul on what you achieved so far. It's not about your age, nor what people think about you. It is only on yourself. Be patient and more kind to yourself.

And finally: think about your technical leadership as your legacy. This is the right moment to start building your own.

This book is part of my legacy. If I can help even a single person to flourish, my time and effort has been spent well.

TAKE AWAY

1. Your only limit is you.

2. Today is the right day to build your legacy.

CHAPTER

SIX DEGREES
OF SEPARATION

SIX DEGREES OF SEPARATION

"A brand is the set of expectations,

memories, stories

and relationships that, taken together,

account for a consumer's decision to choose

one product or service over another."

– Seth Godin

Leadership, branding and the six degrees of separation phenomenon have a lot to do with each other.

The six degrees of separation generally refers back to an experiment performed by S. Milgram [Milgram]: a person needs to send a letter to another without knowing the exact destination address. The only thing he is allowed to do is to pick the best acquaintance he knows that could move the letter a step closer to the destination. The intermediate person would do the same, moving the letter from one hand to the other one until the destination is reached. Milgram ended up showing that we live in a relatively small world., hence concluding that each person is only six steps away from any other person on earth.

How does this experiment relate to technical leadership and your company's brand?

A naïve interpretation is: if you allow your company to gain a bad reputation, this condition will scatter really fast through the world. The bigger the company the more gossiping it generates.

Companies are made of people. And some of them are the decision makers: our leaders. If you - as a company - fail to hold your managers/leaders accountable for how do they do their job, you are in serious trouble. Make your leaders accountable for how they manage their team. How they communicate with people. They are doing a disfavor to your brand and the productivity of the overall company. And it will spread fast.

How long do you think it will take to spread the fact that the company has bad management and culture? Really little, trust me.

And we can prove it even locally. Look at your teams over the time. Consider an unhealthy one. Did you notice how little it takes to generate frictions between you and the members in your team? It takes even less for an unhappy team to start speaking with each other about how bad their experiences and the perceptions of the company are.

People gossiping due to an unhealthy team, is one step closer to generalizing their idea and make it a company-wide opinion. The second one, is one step closer to people speaking with their closer friends about it during their "sad moments". And it can go on and on.

Not saying that it will always happen. But there are good chances for this pattern to be real.

<u>TAKE AWAY</u>

1. Hold your leaders accountable for how they manage – and communicate with - their teams.

2. Bad branding is closer to be spread more than what we might believe.

CHAPTER

CONCLUSION: PUTTING IT ALL TOGETHER

CONCLUSION:
PUTTING IT ALL TOGETHER

I really hope this book has been useful – that you started or improved your journey as a technical leader. In this book I did not try to teach you new theories on how to be successful. My intent has been to share common scenarios and guidance that won't change over time and - when applied – will bring you results. When you are aware of what is going on around you, the journey becomes a little easier.

To be successful you will need to get out of your comfort zone: I totally encourage it. Some of the things discussed so far will require some work to make them stick as a habit. Go back and read again each time you feel you need to: that's part of the learning process. Stick with them until you fully metabolize one piece at the time.

Hear are some final tips for your path to technical leadership:

- Pick your mentors: it does not matter if they are in your company or in your community.
- Books always share the baggage of what people went through in their life: be an avid reader. Authors are 24/7 - almost inexpensive - mentors.
- Brainstorm what you learned: that's the fastest route for improvements.
- Try something new everyday. Don't be scared to make mistakes. See what happens and what works.
- Challenge the status quo and always do your best, the results will come.
- Don't stress about the ultimate big goal, move towards it in small steps. Act daily. Success is made of constant – even slow – actions.

As a final note: build you support network – we all need one. And if you are on this track, you surely have mine!

All the best!

REFERENCES

REFERENCES

[AMAZON PRINCIPLES] Amazon Leadership Principles. Available at: https://www.amazon.jobs/en/principles. Last accessed on September 2018.

[HBR] If your boss could do your job you're more likely to be happy at work. Available at: https://hbr.org/2016/12/if-your-boss-could-do-your-job-youre-more-likely-to-be-happy-at-work. Last Accessed on September 2018.

[MILGRAM] Travers, Jeffrey, and Stanley Milgram. "The small world problem." Psychology Today 1.1 (1967): 61-67.

[PROJECT OXYGEN] Google Great managers still matter: the evolution of Google's Project Oxygen. Available at https://rework.withgoogle.com/blog/the-evolution-of-project-oxygen. Last Accessed on September 2018.

[PETERSON] Dr. Jordan Peterson's. Comprehensive lecture "2017 Personality 04/05: Heroic and Shamanic Initiations"

MORE FROM

GIULIANA CARULLO

MORE FROM GIULIANA CARULLO

Code Reviews 101: The Wisdom of Good Coding

Given her strong background on Software Engineering, Giuliana Carullo shows readers how to perform Code Reviews.

What you will get away from this book is knowledge covering a wide scope of challenges and practices on good coding from code, design and architectural smells to measures, processed and methodologies to perform reviews– the right way. If you want to have some fun, check it out.

ABOUT THE
AUTHOR

ABOUT THE AUTHOR

Giuliana Carullo, CCSK certified, has computer science in her DNA and has been programming for more than a decade. She holds a Master Degree in Computer Science and she's been doing research for the last six years, whilst wearing another hat: the project manager. Giuliana is in love with the intersection point between science and human behavior. She believes that there is more than one way to do good, much more to do bad, but she ends up being really opinionated on what good is.

In her spare time, she loves to write and to help others in doing their best at their jobs, careers and their lives.

THANK YOU!

Made in the USA
Middletown, DE
13 December 2023

45274377R00089